Ova Completa

Ova Completa by Susana Thénon
Copyright © Ediciones Corregidor, 2001, 2021
Translation copyright © Rebekah Smith, 2021
Afterword copyright © María Negroni, 2021
Translator's note copyright © Rebekah Smith, 2021

Originally published in Spanish as *Ova completa*
(Buenos Aires: Editorial Sudamericana, 1987)

Lost Literature Series No. 32

ISBN 978-1-946433-54-1
First Edition, First Printing, 2021

Ugly Duckling Presse
The Old American Can Factory
232 Third Street #E-303
Brooklyn, NY 11215
www.uglyducklingpresse.org

Distributed in the USA by SPD/Small Press Distribution
Distributed in the UK by Inpress Books

Cover design by Ruby Kapka
Typesetting by Doormouse
The type is Hoefler Text

Printed and bound by McNaughton & Gunn

The translation and publication of this book was supported by a grant from the New
York State Council on the Arts with the support of Governor Andrew Cuomo and the
New York State Legislature, along with support from the New York City Department of
Cultural Affairs. This project is supported by the Robert Rauschenberg Foundation and
is published within the framework of "Sur" Translation Support Program of the Ministry
of Foreign Affairs, International Trade and Worship of the Argentine Republic. / Obra
editada en el marco del Programa "Sur" de Apoyo a las Traducciones del Ministerio de
Relaciones Exteriores, Comercio Internacional y Culto de la República Argentina.

Ova Completa

Susana Thénon
translated by Rebekah Smith

Lost Literature Series No. 32

CONTENTS

Ova Completa by Susana Thénon
translated by Rebekah Smith 7

Ova completa by Susana Thénon 67

"*Ova Completa*: A Feast of Meaning"
by María Negroni 129

"The Whole Ova" by Rebekah Smith 135

Translator's Acknowledgments 141

why is that woman screaming?
why is she screaming?
why is that woman screaming?
don't even try to understand

that woman, why is she screaming?
don't even try to understand
look at what beautiful flowers
why is she screaming?
hyacinths   asters
why?
why what?
why is that woman screaming?

and that woman?
and that woman?
just try and understand
she must be crazy that woman
look   look at the little mirrors
could it be because of her steed?
don't even try to understand

and where did you hear
the word steed?
it's a secret   that woman
why is she screaming?
look at the asters
the woman
little mirrors
little birds
that don't sing

why is she screaming?
that don't fly
why is she screaming?
that don't intrude

the woman
and that woman
and was she crazy that woman?

she's not screaming any more

(do you remember that woman?)

you
who've read Dante in folio
you let yourself drift
through those little drawings
so-called illuminated miniatures
and you swallowed it all
all
from ay
to bi

but it's a lie

that hellish bin of complications is pure rubbish
made on purpose to make you waste time
calculating in which circle
the bones of your soul
will end up

and you know something?
this famous inferno
has an admirable simplicity
it's not for nothing, the master's cunning

you get there and they tell you

you're free
go ahead and do as you like

OMNES GENERATIONES

let's go with one in vitro
and one in polyurethane
from Stockholm

I'll educate them as much as possible

I won't educate them

benedice carafam et monitorem
quia mineralia sunt et
penes mineralia burstitur

or better three
in formica
in cobalt

or four or six or a shard in love

Y Vos También

there's saccharine here
the flock of albatross
or what do I know
I mean about albatross
dollars
about albatros dollars
I never saw a bird pishing that's not saying much
the Canadians pish even if you don't see it
and the fish
the fish pish the sea
you're a poet, no?
or Sappho made in Shitland
poetess
don't you see she's a woman?
come on woman
and if you don't get the chance to talk to God
why ask him if I ever?
I'll tell you honestly
in fact
at some time or other I've stopped adoring you
but English is more practical
you make do all over
in other words in the privates
do it   don't
and even if you pronounce it poorly
they'll still understand you
do it   don't
or express yourself with gestures
if you've seen how you do it

how you learn how to *do it*
how you *don't* get used to
how you make *do* how you want
it how you
don't

THE DISSECTION

almost holy thing
is an almost holy thing
a thing almost
almost holy
so almost holy is this thing
that it forcibly draws the attention
the almost absolute blindness of people
taking into account that in the final accounting
it is almost unnecessary to see to believe in a thing so almost
so consequently almost
holy
and what's more this element or thing
has bled
or almost
and we can esteem it from the shade of what's almost bleeding
over the earth over the earth over this exact same earth
and resuming the explanation
we have this thing
a thing bah a ton
of thing almost half holy
and what's more bloody and therefore
and in budding almost *ad nauseam*
and this thing in another order of things
resists with almost all of its buttons
being almost uncovered
analyzed pulverized eviscerated
up to its final internal reasons
better to say almost internal because the thing itself
doesn't peel off so easily

but rather layer by layer
like an artichoke
like winter
and time ah time that disjunctive
factor that almost runs out here
and therefore impedes us
from reaching the great why
and the superhow of this thing
almost holy
so tam tam almost holy
so almost almost
almost so holy

mephitic, you hearest
if I say "mephitic" I have no
choice but to add
"you hearest"
it's a need for refinement
it's elegance: "do you hearest?"
I cannot say to you
"you hearest stinky"
nor "you hearest with a funky stench"
and even less "with a tumbling spuzza you hearest"
just like it would be counterproductive to exclaim,
"yo! toss the roses in the vase!"
it's called language consciousness
intransgression
pavement
that slides into the Monument
lifelong profile in the funerary stele
perhaps offprint frontal lobotomy
it doesn't matter when some day
it doesn't matter how
like iron like chewing gum like screw
you have to be there
do you hearest? there
"mephitic"
it's so easy
you hearest archaic
seest?
taking a chance with "wrecked" or "incontinent"
it's a passport to marginality
whilst you want to be the prize of crackpot anthologies?
to have a wart in the curriculum?

that Erato would fulminate you?
which dung shall you take?
rules precepts laws
rules precepts laws you want
rules precepts laws you want you've got
and decorum currency security
do you hearest?
meanwhile they smell like shit
you emerge mephitic
meanwhile they die wrecked
whilst you expire archaic
you emerge you expire mephitic archaic
mephitic archaic
you expire

the engineers laugh lightly
at the skinny poets

look at them in the reflected light
uncoil them with care

no veins
nor traces
they report

the blue stripe more than petroleum
is a metaphor for water

and the yellow zone does not disclose
neither by-products nor krill

nobody will feed off this
they report

but I advise you not to deactivate them

As Time Goes By (*Yippy te ipsum*)

you go on becoming
in more than one meaning

not like Stearns

you go on becoming young
                  shaggy
                      _____ (you fill it in)
and you can convince yourself and publicize
"I am Me and my Peripherals"

(if you don't like it calm down
YOU CAN STILL CHOOSE
since being the year that it is
we find ourselves in what will be
a certain phase of an unnamed era
in its first segment: age
of the proto-useless options)

if you don't like "and my Peripherals"
you can choose from these leftovers: "and my Kits"
                                        "and my Gadgets"
                                        "and my Accessories"
                                        "and my Tassels"
                                        "and my Replacements"
                                        "and my Trinkets"
                                        "and my Chess Pieces"
                                        "and my Agoraphobics"

which is that which did *not* occur to Socrates but
there is no reason to resemble Socrates
no reason to believe that he knew nothing
except that he was a thorough idiot
(see the Greek "citizen" *idiótes*)

you go on becoming
fear
value
confusing
inhibited
conservative
unpublished
unjustly forgotten
or remembered
even revolutionary you go on becoming

so goes the road
so goes the rule

so goes the so goes the year that is flowing
so goes the so goes the concrete krato
so goes

the great so go the reliefs of martyrdom
and revenge

Non-Stop

to believe that I'm going to India to believe that I understand
what I believe that must be believed

to believe that I understood what must be believed in order to know and
to believe that I'm in India because I believe I know
what must be believed

to believe that I'm still in India to deepen this knowing
without allowing myself to believe I'm illusioned by
some kind of ganges
professor temple cow a million dead bodies
some kind of ganges

to believe that my believing that I'm in India has a cosmic dimension
unrepeatable untranslatable

to believe that my believing that I'm in India will be fundamental
for my believing knowing
and that of India

to believe that still being in India a whole year will resolve the dilemma
of what it is to believe oneself to be a being anxious to know

incidentally to believe that it's my duty to elaborate to handwrite to
    transliterate
to reelaborate and to diffuse

to believe that by now it's time to believe that I seized all that I had
to understand

to believe that by now it's time to return to the longed for homeland
  to spread
so much knowing

to believe to be leaving India to arrive in the longed for homeland
to see to see to be unable to believe

unable to believe
unable to be

to believe that I'm returning to India to see if I understand
what I believe that must be believed

POEM WITH SIMULTANEOUS SPANISH-SPANISH TRANSLATION

> *To go towards what's to come,*
> *to create, if not a paradise,*
> *a happy worker's house*
> *in the fullness of this town,*
> *an intimate bond links*
> *and an external force unites*
> *the race of Anglo-Saxons*
> *with that of Latin Americans.*
>
> Rubén Darío, *Song to Argentina*

Cristóforo
       (the Bearer of Christ)
son of a humble carder of wool
       (son of one who went for weaving without carding)
sailed forth from the port of Poles
       (pole in paw he forsook the port)
not without first persuading Her Majesty the Queen
Isabel the Catholic of the benefits of the enterprise
he'd conceived
       (not without first persuading Su Majestad la Reina
       die Königin Bella the Logistical to cop
       the crown in Blumenthal's con-verted canteen
even if they poured out liters and liters of
genuine ancient B-negative blood
       (even if it cost blood sweat and antipodal
       tears)
went off to sea
       (went to seed)

and after months and months of ingesting only
oxymorons looking for the elusive roundness
  (and after days and days of chewing Yorkshire pudding
  with an extra penguin on Sundays)
someone exclaimed land
  (no one exclaimed thalassa)
they disembarked
in 1492 A.D.
  (treading
  on 1982 A.D.)
chiefs were waiting
genuflecting
in the buff
  (big shots were waiting
  naked
  on their knees)
Cristóforo drew out his missal
  (Christopher shot off his missile)
said to his peers
  (muttered to his stooges)
coño
  (fuck)
behold these new worlds here
  (behold the unworldly filth here)
keep them
  (loot them)
for God and Our Queen
  (for God and Our Queen)
A M E N
  (O M E N)

Tenement Building

dead supers sweep trails of rain

documentary of bulls

remaining greenish

mouth split
plumber or president
they go to lunch they don't return

ludwig van mendelssohn bartholdy

with the slice of a penknife, the yellow woman
makes two sons of one

Ova Completa*

Philosophy means "rape of a living being."
It comes from the Greek *philoso*, "which cuts deep,"
and *phia*, the 3rd person of the verb *phiar*, which is
"to trust" and also "to give on credit *ad referendum*."
Those who practice this activity are called *friends*
or the "Brotherhood of the Smiling,"
the bondsmen—certainly—
those who really have a grip on it and those who think they do
in the colossal mosque of Al-Hopeso

Once the philosophy is consummated
the following appear in this order:

the taqueria the deputy the judge of the case
the forensic agent the public defender the photojournalist
the sealed brief Max Scheler a neighboring family
a psychiatrist two guards

And within that, there are:

1 who mislaid her legs 1 priest
1 indifferent observer 1 sadist 1 Racing team sticker fanatic
1 (ONE) copy of the Children's Illustrated Erasmus

And there's more,
deeper in:

the memory of a famous phrase the forgetting of that
famous phrase after which follows the forgetting of all that is

famous and that is not except for your ass

Philosophy means "rape of a living being."

when your sentence is commuted 26 years later
take up the drills again or they'll drill you

*OVA: Latin; plural neutral noun. Literally: eggs.
COMPLETA: Latin; passive plural neutral participle in agreement
with eggs. Literally: abundant. Possible variants: filled,
full, brimming, swollen.

if you were to sleep in Ramos Mejía
my love
what a disaster it would be

how I'd be at the soles of your feet
how I'd wait for a streetcar
how arriving at night
I'd board at midday

what a disaster it would be

with your estranged grandma
with your sister and her manias
with your cousins the captains
we're keeping company

what a disaster it would be

with your mother and the window
with your mother night and day
with your mother who makes us
a bed black with ants

what a disaster it would be

without your hollows in my hollows
without your shadows in mine
without fingers to beat
my agony's drum

if you were to sleep in Ramos Mejía
my love
what a disaster it would be

what a disaster it would be

beloved

my love

THE FUNDS OF THE TREASURY

to get to the funds of the Treasury
you first have to find a Treasure
and go in through the door
or even through the window
or slide a kid through the cracks
or creep across the rusty skylights
half-open
maybe half-closed

the Treasury is taking a siesta
having left saying
"if anyone calls tell them I'm taking a siesta"
"even if it's the minister?"
"even if that"
I am the Treasury
and I have become a fabulous animal

of course I'm not featured in the *Fantastic Zoolo
guide of Borges*
but I'll feature in the next editions
as *addenda*
as breaking news
or as asterisk fodder

a fabulous animal
that grows while it sleeps

if they wake it up
or touch it

or try to change its place
it shrinks to the point of disappearing
and reappears years later in remote latitudes
where the cycle is completed relentlessly
by man's action
which is the kindling of history
and therefore the charcoal of time

sleeping I grow gigantic
and waking I die

everyone talks about the funds
and everyone fights to play in them
they play craps   they play hide-and-seek
in vain it's discovered that such funds
are like the Caucasus
a place that only exists
for the Caucasians
and documentary screenwriters
there is no way to reach them
without waking up my siesta
and evaporating me
with funds fronts and a dividing wall

that they'd leave me in peace
if they want peace
but if they want something else
they'll have it in abundance
fat cows are sheer fat
while skinny cows move lightly
and can even whistle

I am the Treasury
a fabulous animal
don't touch me
dedicate yourselves to ahrt
speak of the mystic
and of the semantic
meditate beneath the pyramid
have a lot to do
life ahead
death ahead
and both on your sides
up high
and inside

philosophize
archive
hang heads of garlic

I am the Treasury

sleeping I grow gigantic
and waking I die

leave me in peace

struss
one of the great evils
that affect womanity
before it was called stress
and before that strass
or Strauss
it's like a stumbling waltz
for the woman without a shadow
there is no drama
she's drunk
drunk the pig

struss

you've considered killing
and you feel horrible

you've considered killing
and you feel horrible

whom?

you've considered
you consider
killing

you keep calibrating considering reconsidering contemplating conceiving
eliminating a solid body that moreover expels carbonic anhydride
from its nostrils
a body that as you understand it
is surplus
impedes respiration
and contaminates
a pocket-sized nuclear reactor
relative *brevitatis causa*
bad friend
creditor
functionary
viscount
lousy novelist
my mother
tennis champion
unknown fragrant green phantasmal
good friend
your very own body

the condominium

you've considered killing
syllables
whistles
corpses

how great to kill corpses

for easter I'll make them an inferno
with special cotillion service
surprise in the vault!
magic clowns gumballs clepsydra digital pyrotechnics
for easter
maybe for epiphany

some carry a rosary in their hands
others a book
others a bouquet of chard
I carry a Colt from a John Wayne movie

you've considered killing a body more or less formed
your error is in the calculation
you start with just one corpse
and go on to thousands
there's no end to this round

I warm up the Colt
it serves as a stove
I write or I don't
I feel horrible or I don't

I've dreamt clenched
since I lost my teeth

you've considered killing
I've considered killing
let's warm up the Colt
the Smith & Wesson
the grenade in the sewer in Monte Grande

are there more bullets than bodies?
more bodies than bullets?

come and drink a tea
or don't come

I'm considering killing
I'm doing my work for tomorrow

I'm leaving
and they've already come back

PRESTIGE: former rest stop
en route to the grand terminus STYX LAGOON

it is possible to get off
but you run the risk of forever becoming a
schizoid toad: a being that jumpily
survives the changes in the tracks

in PRESTIGE there are also sandwiches
in case hunger forecloses your future

eat as much as you like

don't go looking at the filling

great alchemy lies only in daybreak

`

Pholl Stop (Tango with Critical Vector)

"the cattleprod in the closet
 is hanging there still
 nobody ever amputates anything
 or makes its volts vibrate"

THIS IS DECLAMATION!

no

in a filthy dark room that I never leave that
I never enter where I always am not or I am crying or spitting
urinating writing crawling or speaking speaking to the painting a
room of crazy ancestors blacklegs usurers assassins suicides
beggars thieves solemn swollen in a dark room
of blood of shadow in a room where if I am I'm not
or I am who cares and waiting for everything outside inside
in a room with walls of the dead dead dead who leap out
of dreams they eat you in a room upstairs where I'm writing to you
convulsions of a dead woman and a dead man of a dead son of a bitch like all
the dead and their parents grandparents and nephews like all the dead women
a red room rotten with blood through their eyes a room
yours the neighbor's where I am or am not or you were or would be
or they were without day with a window onto the black background onto the wall of
mucous onto the abyss coagulated with sperm in a room of art of
the pure artist of seraphic filth parisian florentine scoundrel a
room of a scoundrel more scoundrel than dead like all the dead
and the women and the children first like all the dead from
across and from the corner and from the northeast in a room of
an incorruptible artist dead decorated and dead and tidy and
educated where I am or am not look what happens and dead woman and dead man
in a room of a dead sick healthy trodden-on famous artist
in a room of a child child ancestor sickly yellow from
masturbating against all the motherly human and divine of a dead
artist and father and pride of the school in a room brown and
filthy my eternity the eternity where the soul is scraped down to

the bone to find to find that word that ineffable
immortal sponger in order to lie in order to swindle

"in the star . . ."

La Musik

a German man came
saw
and immediately founded the
Concentus Musicus Araucanus

one day I up and said
maybe I'll go see a concert

they played a sonata in C flat
for two harps and wild panflute

I put on an organza trench coat
and a spritz of French extract
that I've had since the First World War

I took the 106
I went a block too far
didn't matter it was early
the bell on the 106 went ring-a-ling
a sad old woman asked me, are you exiting?
no *señora*
I'm getting off

I went back a block
when I arrived all that was left was
Paradise behind the column
well alright
it's better than nothing and to dust you'll return

the program said ritornelli
cantorum danse macabre
and again it said ritornelli
what have I come for
and Kyrie Gloria

hold on tight
this is culture
which means:
that some turned the fields and out came plants
and others turned their encephalons and out came
the brothers Karamazov

that's what they said to Cookie
who studies Letters

they also told her other things
but the concert had already started
and I am here to talk about the concert

and I really love talking about concerts
it's much more cultural than showing slides
of Firenze and saying, "remember, Carlos,
when you lost your shoe in the Baptistry?"

why is it
that those who play the harp are always women

in green tunics they flanked
the one with the panflute
a skinny man in black
who looked like Leguisamo

the concert wasn't bad
not bad at all
the pizzicato is a beauty
said the guy next to me to the woman just beyond him
and he also said contrapunto ricercare
and bell (the one on the 106 goes ring-a-ling)
and added cantus firmus and Guillaume de Machaut

meanwhile I don't know why
the skinny man in black
who looked like Leguisamo
reminded me of the casino
(I would say "of Montecarlo" but I don't know how to lie)
in Miramar

no more bets Leguisamo ululated
under the ritornelli of the chips
the danse macabre of zero
and the firmus firmus tapestry
like the rock of Tarpeia   (it's the culture)
that rhymes with Pompeya   (it's the culture)
and with the blond Mireya   (of the *élite* and popular)

in the end
you'll all have seen
that Musik doesn't only tame the beasts
but also
makes the chickens crazy
favors the association of ideas
and allows you to stretch out on the couch
and talk about the concert

okay so
I'm dead
and I want to have fun

come on
where is everyone?

no one's here?

yes
yes
a beam of light comes through the window

I'm outside
and you're inside
playing with the mirror

you cover my eye with sun

well done
because I'm dead
and I want to have fun

can I come in now?
not yet?

I should wait?
like before?
a little more?

like before

the mirrors
the sun

I'm outside
you're inside

not yet?

INTERMISSION

and when there's nowhere left
to mend them
and they don't protect from the night
from the witchy dread
from death and her jokes

and when there is no
soul left in which to vomit
your loaves of bread
your convictions
your armistices and dismissals
your asylums
where you bandaged the world
with phylacteries
of hate

in half-red panties
your heart bleeds

(seven of veils:
hang the stockings
from the porthole manna plummets
easter boils
families chafe
tribes prostrate
clans toast with heroes
heroes with megasimians)

and when there's nowhere left
to mend them
and your jellyfish open up into tatters
the rusty trunk creaks
behind the eyelid

the spring leaps
you've finally arrived
on the wings of the void
dressed up like a little white bunny

do you remember
those winter nights
with the radiant sun?
star king they called it?
don't answer me

how we thought then:
"why waste time?"
scarcely centuries
and a poorly collated
instruction manual

and so as not to waste it
—time—
we went from the shroud
into old age
and from there to middle age

and so as not to waste it
we invented
the holy war
of scraping the tongue against the teeth
a palatal storm

and still I remember
the little houses with no street
the triangular cats
abstract from hunger
around the day

you too remember
only you've moved on so much
while I was talking
that you arrived at the bib
and you're drenching comfortable fogs
in sound

to your health little girl

don't stop to wait for me
the rhetoric is my problem

when I find some happy ending
—and I almost found it—
I'm going to clamber up
to your silence
to share it

and if I still have legs
I'll crawl to my cradle

MOHAMMED KAFKA, BOOKSELLER

"O Thyself?"
"sold out
100,000 copies in two months"
"and *Cowself?*"
"in a bilingual edition
Coptic-Hungarian
with the Coptic it's possible
there are some courses
they say it's very close to Québecois
of course
nothing like *Cowself* in middle Saxon
but it flew
plain and simple
not even one left
I can offer you instead
Avellaneda's *Quixote*"
"What am I to do with *Cowself?*"
"or complutensian porn
12th century *you know*
and then I have on sale
a batch of Arthur Hailey's *Opera Omnia* in paperback
and *The Parallel Lives Onanimize*
by Pseudo Plutonium and as if that were not enough
two pocket combs a corkscrew a
stamp of Luther

for today only"

I am the little fish

I'm going for your teeth

all my affairs are in order

there is no way to alter my destiny
as proverb

I'm bringing an entrail, rich with
virus
mercury
your tasty great-grandsons

I am the little fish

I'm coming

there is no way to alter
your destiny
as proverb

Dreadful Western Sequence with Equanimous Chinese Ending

a birth means wanting everything
and fussing and fussing

a growing up means wanting a lot
and fussing with oneself and fussing

maturing means wanting something
and fussing not to be getting it

oldening means wanting little
and fussing a bit more each time

and dying means wanting nothing
and fussing a bit less each time

KIKIRIKYRIE

god help us or god don't help us
or god half help us
or he makes us believe that he'll help us
and later sends word that he's busy
or he helps us obliquely
with a pious "help yourself"
or cradles us in his arms singing softly that we'll pay for it
if we don't go to sleep immediately
or whispers to us that here we are today and oh tomorrow too
or tells us the story of the cheek
and the one about the neighbor and the one about the leper
and the one about the little lunatic and the one about the mute who talked
or he puts in his headphones
or shakes us violently roaring that we'll pay for it
if we don't wake up immediately
or gives us the tree test
or takes us to the zoo to see
how we look at ourselves
or points out an old train on a ghost of a bridge
propped up by posters for disposable diapers

god help us or not or halfway
or haltingly

god us
god what
or more or less
or neither

THE ANTHOLOGY

are you
the great poietisa
Susana Etcetera?
nice to meet you
my name is Petrona Smith-Jones
I'm an assistant professor
at the University of Poughkeepsie
which is just a weensie bit south of Vancouver
and I'm in Argentina
on a Putifar grant
to put together an anthology
of developing, developed,
and also menopausal writers
although it's well-known that at any rate
all those that wrote and will write in Argentina
are already part of the '60s generation
including those in daycare
and even most including those in assisted living

but what is deeply important to me
in the poetry of you and your peers
is that profession—ahhh, how to put it?—
that profusion of icons and indices
what do you think about the icon?
do women all use it
or is it also a macho thing?

because, you know, in reality
what interests me

is not only that they write
but that they're feminists
and if possible alcoholics
and if possible anorexics
and if possible rape victims
and if possible lesbians
and if possible very very unhappy

this will be a democratic anthology
but please don't bring me
the independent or sane

"where is the exit?"
"excuse me?"
"I asked where the exit was."
"no
 there is no exit."
"but how, if I came in?"
"of course
 I remember you
 and what's more I'm looking at you
 but an exit
 there's no exit,
 you see?"
"but that can't be
 I'm going to leave the way I came in"
"no
 it's already quite late
 entry is prohibited after ten
 and anyway, what do you want? that I put my neck on the line
 to let someone leave
 through the entrance?"
"listen
 there has to be some way of getting outside"
"did you ask at information?"
"yes,
 but they sent me to you"
"okay then
 and I tell you that there is no exit"
"where is there a telephone?"
"to call whom?"
"the police"
"this is the police"

"what are you crazy? this is a concert
 hall"
"yes, until a certain time
 then it's the police"
"and what's going to happen to me?"
"it depends who's on duty
 if it's Loiácono
 it's a free ride
 you'll be out in just a few days"
"but this is insane
 where are the other people?"
"confined sector
 first sub-basement"
"why
 are you doing
 this?"
"come on auntie
 don't tell me you've never been to a concert"

MURGATORY

olé olé
olé olá
I am the grandson
of my papa

olé olé
olé olá
going to the pisschologist
to probe away

why oh why
pour quoi pour quoi
la vie en rose
is not pour moi

perhaps perhaps
could be could be
this must be seen in
profundity

molta lettura
molta poesia
molta cultura
molta pazzia

Nevsky Stogorny
Drugoi Igrushky
Gogol Andreyev
Chekhov Tiburshky

and when I learned
my perspective
I found myself
in Intensive

man of science
man of the world
oh great master
oh dirty old bastard

you knew it all
could do it all
but now you've seen
it's no joke at all

olé olé
olé olá
no one with   brains in
the great
be

here

ROUND 15

oh yes
easy
word games
tampon of such voices
preventsme
swal
low
ing

easier than not doing
or doing nothing
like god's uncle

like god's uncle
who didn't do anything

flying fromthealph abet

I'm drowning

that thing that was called that other thing
is now "this"
alias "something"
alias "the thing"
and in the lapse that goes from the second line to the one before
the same bartered for the same
and "this" goes on with more
with peroxide

an ululating ton of who knows what
has gotten together
in front of the church

that thing that was called that other thing
is now "this"

and in the end was the Name

LIBRETTOS

I

homerican rhapsody

from Saint Petersburg
the Great Four
rubricate another armistice
Simeon and Volodia are arrested
for spray painting *graffiti*
Simeon and Volodia are shot
in the parlors of Castel Gandolfo
His Holiness the Pope
midges meanwhile a chamberlain
cleans fixes and grants splendor
spreading black pox black plague black widow
in the *New York Times* a psychic proclaims
that such epidemics will one day be called
silly pox pink plague and merry widow
another psychic predicts the return to the future
Juan Cruz Montejo dies matures grows
is born in Paysandú
crawling through the corridors
the Great Four
play with a slingshot
nuclear yo-yo
genitals pruned by the old woman
(this will be understood
says the third psychic
with the advent of some Sigmundo

or Segismundo)
in Glasgow it's snowing
in Tunis it's partly cloudy
midges A.D. the Pope His Holiness
in the gardens of Castel Gandolfo
the cardinals warble for longer and better
anger gluttony envy pride lust
etcetera avarice and adultery
666 wins the final round
from the casements
the Great Four
give free passage
to every poetconsul
and/or Nobel-bard

look what's in the sky
I don't see anything
look what's on the ground
I don't see anything
look what's in the water in the fire
I don't see anything

in Troy the sun's coming out

I don't see anything

II

the second parting

begins
and begins
and begins

the age of laughter

give me a kiss (you)
infect me (right now! now!
curved foyers from the other world!)

CONSUME MORE HOST MORE CRIME

taking into account the extension of the polar night
I would have said to you: The rooster will not crow
without you having denied me three hundred times three

and besides—it's unnecessary to emphasize it—
it is what you did

of course according to A. Camus I knew myself to be indirectly responsible
in the matter of Herod and "all children under the age of two
that were in Bethlehem and all its surrounding areas."
but that doesn't justify you
although ultimately who really cares
the libretto is how it is
have to keep up with it

now lend me a worm

now lend me a kiss on the cheek
now put your hand on my gangrenes
now cry
and now console yourself
dreaming that I'll soon be back
and *your* horrific sacrifices
will earn you my right hand

stone   stone
(over this stone)
sandstone
I abandon you to the librettos of time

III

the second waiting

the means for securing love having run out
(:pliable element in the shape of a bowtie)
the Way of Truth arises
whose transit isn't easy
but yes inevitable
as it is inevitable
to survive the . . mbs
look at the Japanese the cockroach
brot . ers of the world
we need blankets vaccines
vacuum cleaners powdered mi . .
. . . . tarv . . .   .
w . nee . plasma rancor and diet whiskey

brothers of the world
fortunate Abels
we need everything
except logos

. . . .
. . . .
erect

. . . .
. . . .
ruin(s) . . . .
make of a new world a
v . . erable site
l . . 's . . fo . .
. . . . yogurt
. . . .
craters in the sea . . tacombs
new . . . . rotten
flem . . . plagues
more art
more dep . . . . . .
. . ofessoriate
more irony, *darling*

from this Tree
you don't choose . . . . there is no story
follow the lib . . . . .
peck from the other one
. ndelible vagina birth the dead
who build

Ova completa

Susana Thénon

¿por qué grita esa mujer?
¿por qué grita?
¿por qué grita esa mujer?
andá a saber

esa mujer ¿por qué grita?
andá a saber
mirá que flores bonitas
¿por qué grita?
jacintos   margaritas
¿por qué?
¿por qué qué?
¿por qué grita esa mujer?

¿y esa mujer?
¿y esa mujer?
vaya a saber
estará loca esa mujer
mirá   mirá los espejitos
¿será por su corcel?
andá a saber

¿y dónde oíste
la palabra corcel?
es un secreto   esa mujer
¿por qué grita?
mirá las margaritas
la mujer
espejitos
pajaritas
que no cantan

¿por qué grita?
que no vuelan
¿por qué grita?
que no estorban

la mujer
y esa mujer
¿y estaba loca esa mujer?

ya no grita

(¿te acordás de esa mujer?)

vos
que leíste a Dante en fascículos
te dejaste llevar
por esos dibujitos
a los que llaman miniaturas iluminadas
y te tragaste todo
todo
de pe
a pu

pero es mentira

ese complicadero del infierno es pura macana
hecha a propósito para hacerte perder tiempo
en calcular a qué círculo irán a dar
los huesos de tu alma

¿y sabés una cosa?
este famoso averno
es de una sencillez admirable
que no de balde su señor es astuto

llegás allí y te dicen

sos libre
andá y hacé lo que te dé la gana

OMNES GENERATIONES

que marchen uno in vitro
y una in poliuretano
de Estocolmo

los educaré como pueda

no los educaré

benedice garrafam et monitorem
quia mineralia sunt et
penes mineralia revententur

o mejor tres
in fórmica
in cobalto

o cuatro o seis o esquirla enamorada

AND SO ARE YOU

hay sacarina
la bandada de albatros
o yo qué sé
digo de albatros
dólares
*de albatros*dólares
nunca vi un pájaro pishar eso no quiere decir nada
los canadienses pishan aunque vos no los veas
y los peces
los peces pishan mar
vos sos poeta ¿no?
o Sappho made in Shitland
poetisa
¿no ves que es mujer?
vamos mujer
si no puedes tú con Dios hablar
¿para qué preguntarle si yo alguna vez?
te lo digo personalmente
en efecto
alguna que otra vez te he dejado de adorar
pero el inglés es más práctico
te ingeniás en todas partes
verbigracia en las pudendas
do it   don't
y aunque pronuncies mal
igual te entienden
do it   don't
o te expresás por señas
vieras cómo te arreglás

73

cómo aprendés a *do it*
cómo *don't* te acostumbrás
cómo hacés *do* lo que querés
it cómo
don't

LA DISECCIÓN

cosa casi sagrada
es una cosa casi sagrada
una cosa casi
casi sagrada
tan casi sagrada es esta cosa
que llama poderosamente la atención
la casi absoluta ceguera de la gente
para tener en cuenta que a fin de cuentas
es casi innecesario ver para creer en cosa tan casi
tan consecuentemente casi
sagrada
y es que además este elemento o cosa
ha sangrado
o casi
y podemos apreciarlo por la sombra de lo casi sangrado
sobre el suelo sobre el suelo sobre el mismísimo suelo
y retomando la demostración
tenemos esta cosa
una cosa bah el montón
de cosa casi medio sagrada
y además sangrada y por ende
y en ciernes casi *ad nauseam*
y cn otro orden de cosas esta cosa
se resiste con casi todos sus botones
a ser casi descubierta
analizada remolida destripada
en sus causales últimos internos
mejor dicho casi internos porque la cosa en sí
no se deshoja fácilmente

sino capa tras capa
como los alcauciles
los inviernos
y el tiempo ah el tiempo ese factor
disyuntivo que casi aquí se agota
y por lo tanto nos impide
llegar al gran por qué
y al supercómo de esta cosa
casi sagrada
tam tam casi sagrada
tan casi casi
casi tan sagrada

mefítico oís vosotros
si digo "mefítico" no tengo
más remedio que añadir
"oís vosotros"
es mester de finura
es galanura ¿oís vosotros?
yo no os puedo decir
"apestoso oís vosotros"
ni "con olor a mufa oís vosotros"
y menos "con una spuzza que volteaba oís vosotros"
así como sería contraproducente exclamar
"¡meté las rosas en el búcaro ché!"
se llama conciencia de lengua
intransgresión
pavimento
que desliza al Monumento
perfil vitalicio en la estela funeraria
tal vez separata lobotomía frontal
no importa cuándo algún día
no importa cómo
como fierro como chicle como tuerca
hay que estar ahí
¿oís vosotros? ahí
"mefítico"
es tan fácil
vetusto oís vosotros
¿véis?
arriesgarse con "choto" o "chacabuco"
es pasaporte a la marginación
¿queréis ser presa de antólogos chiflados?
¿tener una verruga en el currículum?

¿que Erato os fulmine?
¿qué boñiga queréis?
reglas preceptos leyes
reglas preceptos leyes queréis
reglas preceptos leyes queréis tenéis
y decoro pecunia seguridad
¿oís vosotros?
mientras ellos tienen olor a mierda
vosotros devenís mefíticos
mientras ellos mueren chotos
vosotros fenecéis vetustos
devenís fenecéis mefíticos vetustos
mefíticos vetustos
fenecéis

los ingenieros ríen suavemente
de los poetas flacos

los miran al trasluz
los desenrollan con delicadeza

no hay vetas
ni vestigios
informan

la franja azul más que petróleo
es metáfora del agua

y la zona amarilla no revela
subproducto ni krill

nadie comerá de esto
informan

pero aconsejo no desactivarlos

SEGÚN PASAN LOS AÑOS (GOZQUE TE IPSUM)

te vas volviendo
en más de un sentido

no como Stearns

te vas volviendo joven
                    peludo
                    ------- (llenalo vos)
y podés convencerte y divulgar
"Yo soy Yo y mis Periféricos"

(si no te gusta calmate
PODÉS ELEGIR TODAVIA
pues siendo el año que es
nos encontramos en lo que será
cierta fase de una era innominada
en su primer segmento: evo
de las opciones protoinútiles)

si no te gusta "y mis Periféricos"
podés elegir entre estos saldos: "y mis Kits"
                                    "y mis Gadgets"
                                    "y mis Accesorios"
                                    "y mis Caireles"
                                    "y mis Repuestos"
                                    "y mis Abalorios"
                                    "y mis Trebejos"
                                    "y mis Agorafobios"

que es lo que *no* le occurría a Sócrates pero
no hay por qué parecerse a Sócrates
ni por qué creer que no sabía nada
salvo que era un cabal idiota
(véase el griego *idiótes* 'ciudadano')

te vas volviendo
miedo
valor
confuso
abatatada
conservador
inédita
injustamente olvidado
o recordada
hasta revolucionario te vas volviendo

según el camino
según el canon

según el según del año que fluye
según el según del krato concreto
según

el gran según de los relevos de martirio
y revancha

NON STOP

creer que voy a la India a creer que entiendo
lo que creo que hay que creer

creer que entendí lo que hay que creer para saber y
creer que estoy en la India porque creo saber
lo que hay que creer

creer que sigo en la India para profundizar este saber
sin permitirme creer que me ilusiona
ganges alguno
profesor templo vaca millón de muertos
ganges alguno

creer que mi creer estar en India tiene un sentido cósmico
irrepetible intraducible

creer que mi creer estar en India será fundamental
para mi creer saber
y el de la India

creer que el seguir en India todo un año resolverá el dilema
de lo que es creerse un ser ansioso de saber

de paso creer que es mi deber elaborar manuscribir trasliterar
reelaborar y difundir

creer que ya es hora de creer que capté todo lo que había que
entender

creer que ya es hora de volver a la añorada patria a divulgar
tanto saber

creer salir de la India llegar a la añorada patria
ver ver no poder creer

no poder creer
no poder ser

creer que vuelvo a la India a ver si entiendo
lo que creo que hay que creer

Poema con traducción simultánea español-español

Para ir hacia lo venidero,
para hacer, si no el paraíso,
la casa feliz del obrero
en la plenitud ciudadana,
vínculo íntimo eslabona
e ímpetu exterior hermana
a la raza anglosajona
con la latinoamericana.

Rubén Darío, *Canto a la Argentina*

Cristóforo
      (el Portador de Cristo)
hijo de un humilde cardador de lana
      (hijo de uno que iba por lana sin cardar)
zarpó del puerto de Palos
      (palo en zarpa dejó el puerto)
no sin antes persuadir a Su Majestad la Reina
Isabel la Católica de las bondades de la empresa
por él concebida
      (no sin antes persuadir a Her Royal Highness
      die Königin Chabela la Logística de empeñar
      la corona en el figón de Blumenthal con-verso)
así se vertiesen litros y litros de
genuina sangre vieja factor RH negativo
      (así costase sangre sudor y lágrimas
      antípodas)
se hicieron a la mar
      (se hicieron alamares)

y tras meses y meses de yantar solo
oxímoron en busca de la esquiva redondez
        (y tras días y días de mascar Yorkshire pudding
        y un pingüino de añadidura los domingos)
alguno exclamó tierra
        (ninguno exclamó thálassa)
desembarcaron
en 1492 a. D.
        (pisaron
        en 1982 a. D.)
jefes esperaban
en pelota
genuflexos
        (mandamases aguardaban
        desnudos
        de rodillas)
Cristóforo gatilló el misal
        (Christopher disparó el misil)
dijo a sus pares
        (murmuró a sus secuaces)
coño
        (fuck)
ved aquí nuevos mundos
        (ved aquí estos inmundos)
quedáoslos
        (saqueadlos)
por Dios y Nuestra Reina
        (por Dios y Nuestra Reina)
A M É N
        (O M E N)

CASA DE PISOS

porteros muertos barren colas de lluvia

documental de toros

estarse verdoso

boca rajada
plomero o presidente
van a almorzar no vuelven

ludwig van mendelssohn bartholdy

de un navajazo la mujer amarilla
hace de su hijo dos

Ova completa*

Filosofía significa 'violación de un ser viviente'.
Viene del griego *filoso*, 'que corta mucho',
y *fía*, 3a. persona del verbo *fiar*, que quiere decir
'confiar' y también 'dar sin cobrar *ad referendum*'.
Ejercen esta actividad los llamados *friends*
o "Cofradía de los Sonrientes",
los fiadores —desde luego—,
los que de veras tienen la manija y los que creen tenerla
en la descomunal mezquita de Oj-Alá.

Una vez consumada la filosofía
se hacen presentes por orden de aparición:

la taquería el comisario el juez de la causa
el forense el abogado de oficio el reportero gráfico
el secreto del sumario Max Scheler una familia vecina
un psiquiatra dos guardias

Ya adentro, hay:

1 que perdió entrambas gambas 1 sacerdote
1 indiferente 1 sádico 1 calcomaníaco de Racing
1 (UN) ejemplar del Erasmo Ilustrado para Niños

Ya más,
ya bien adentro:

el recuerdo de una frase famosa el olvido de esa
frase famosa al que sigue el olvido de todo lo

famoso y lo que no lo es salvo tu culo

Filosofía significa 'violación de un ser viviente'.

cuando tu pena es condonada 26 años después
retomás su ejercicio o te lo ejercen

*OVA: sustantivo plural neutro latino. Literalmente: huevos.
COMPLETA: participio pasivo plural neutro latino en concordancia
con huevos. Literalmente: colmados. Variantes posibles: rellenos,
repletos, rebosantes, henchidos.

si durmieras en Ramos Mejía
amada mía
qué despelote sería

cómo fuera yo a tus plantas
cómo esperara tranvías
cómo por llegar de noche
abordara a mediodía

qué despelote sería

con tu abuela enajenada
con tu hermana y sus manías
con tus primos capitanes
haciéndonos compañía

qué despelote sería

con tu madre en la ventana
con tu madre noche y día
con tu madre que nos tiende
su cama negra de hormigas

qué despelote sería

sin tus huecos en mis huecos
sin tus sombras en las mías
sin dedos con que golpear
el tambor de la agonía

si durmieras en Ramos Mejía
amada mía
qué despelote sería

qué despelote sería

amada

amada mía

LOS FONDOS DEL TESORO

para llegar a los fondos del Tesoro
hay que encontrar primero un Tesoro
y entrar por la puerta
o bien por la ventana
o deslizar un chico por la grieta
o reptar claraboyas herrumbradas
semiabiertas
tal vez semicerradas

el Tesoro duerme la siesta
ya dejó dicho
—si alguien llama le dices que duermo siesta
—¿aunque sea el ministro?
—aunque lo sea
soy el Tesoro
y he devenido un animal fabuloso

cierto que no figuro en el *Manual de zoolo*
guía fantástica de Borges
pero figuraré en ediciones próximas
como *addenda*
como noticia de último momento
o como carne de asterisco

un animal fabuloso
que crece mientras duerme

si lo despiertan
o lo tocan

o pretenden cambiarlo de lugar
se achica hasta desaparecer
y reaparece años después en latitudes remotas
donde el ciclo se cumple inexorablemente
por acción del hombre
que es madera de la historia
y por lo tanto carbón del tiempo

al dormir me agiganto
y al despertar me muero

todos hablan de los fondos
y todos pugnan por jugar en ellos
a los dados   a la escondida
vanamente descubren que tales fondos
son como el Cáucaso
un lugar que solo existe
para los caucasianos
y los guionistas de documentales
no hay forma de alcanzarlos
sin despertar mi siesta
y evaporarme
con fondos frentes y pared medianera

que me dejen en paz
si quieren paz
pero si quieren otra cosa
la tendrán en abundancia
las vacas gordas son pura grasa
mientras las vacas flacas andan ligero
y hasta pueden silbar

soy el Tesoro
un animal fabuloso
no me toquen
dedíquense al ahrte
hablen de mística
y semántica
mediten debajo de la pirámide
tienen tanto que hacer
la vida por delante
la muerte por delante
y ambas por los costados
por arriba
y por adentro

filosofen
archiven
cuelguen ajos

soy el Tesoro

al dormir me agiganto
y al despertar me muero

déjenme en paz

el struss
uno de los grandes males
que afectan a la womanidad
antes se llamaba stress
y antes strass
o Strauss
es como un vals trastabillado
por la mujer sin sombra
no hay drama
está borracha
borracha la puerca

el struss

has pensado en matar
y te sentís horrible

has pensado en matar
y te sentís horrible

¿a quién?

has pensado
pensás
en matar

venís pesando pensando repensando sopesando sopensando
eliminar un sólido que además expele anhídrido carbónico
desde los ollares
un sólido que a tu entender
está de sobra
impide la respiración
y contamina
un reactor nuclear de bolsillo
brevitatis causa pariente
mal amigo
acreedor
funcionario
vizconde
novelista de cuarta
madre de mí
campeón de tenis
desconocida verde fragante fantasmal
buen amigo
tu propio cuerpo

el condominio

has pensado en matar
sílabas
silbos
muertos

qué bueno matar muertos

para pascua les armaré un infierno
con servicio de cotillón
¡sorpresa en la bóveda!
magia payaso chicle globo clepsidra digital pirotecnia
para pascua
tal vez para reyes

unos llevan rosario entre las manos
otros un libro
otros un hato de acelga
yo un Colt de película de John Wayne

has pensado en matar un sólido más o menos estructurado
tu error está en el cálculo
partís de un solo muerto
y siguen miles
no hay fin para esta ronda

caliento el Colt
sirve de estufa
escribo o no
me siento horrible o no

sueño a regañadientes
desde que no tenía dientes

has pensado en matar
he pensado en matar
calentemos el Colt
el Smith & Wesson
la granada en la cloaca de Monte Grande

¿hay más balas que sólidos?
¿más sólidos que balas?

vení a tomar un té
o no vengas

pienso en matar
hago el deber para mañana

ya me voy
y ya vuelven

PRESTIGIO: apeadero anterior
a la gran terminal LAGUNA ESTIGIA

es posible bajarse
pero corrés el riesgo de volverte por siempre
sapo esquizoide: ser que saltonamente
sobrevive a los cambios de las vías

en PRESTIGIO también hay sandwiches
por si el hambre te cierra el porvenir

comé cuanto quieras

no vayas a mirar el relleno

la magna alquimia solo está en los albores

PUNTO FONAL (TANGO CON VECTOR CRÍTICO)

"la picana en el ropero
 todavía está colgada
 nadie en ella amputa nada
 ni hace sus voltios vibrar"

¡*ESO* ES DECLAMACIÓN!

no

en una pieza oscura y mugrienta de la que nunca salgo a la que nunca entro donde siempre no estoy o estoy llorando escupiendo orinando escribiendo reptando o hablando hablando al cuadro una pieza de antepasados locos tahúres usureros asesinos suicidas pordioseros ladrones solemnes tumefactos en una pieza oscura de sangre de la sombra en una pieza donde si estoy no estoy o estoy a quién le importa y esperándolo todo afuera adentro en una pieza con paredes de muertos muertos muertos que saltan de los sueños te comen en una pieza arriba donde te escribo convulsiones de muerta y muerto de muerto hijo de puta como todos los muertos y sus padres abuelos y sobrinos como todas las muertas una pieza de roja podredumbre de sangre por los ojos una pieza la tuya la de al lado donde estoy o no estoy o estabas o estarías o estuvieron sin día con ventana al fondo negro al paredón de mucus al vacío coagulado de esperma en una pieza de arte de artista puro de seráfica roña parisiense florentina canalla una pieza de canalla más canalla que muerto como todos los muertos y las mujeres y los niños primero como todos los muertos de enfrente y de la esquina y del noreste en una pieza de insobornable artista muerto condecorado y muerto y pulcro y educada donde estoy o no estoy a ver qué pasa y muerta y muerto en una pieza de artista muerto enferma sano pisoteada famoso en una pieza de antepasado niño niño amarillo enteco de masturbarse contra todo lo madremente humano y divino de artista muerto y padre y pundonor de la escuela en una pieza parda y roñosa mi eternidad la eternidad donde se rasca el alma hasta

el hueso para buscar para buscar esa palabra esa inefable
garrapata inmortal para mentir para embaucar

"en la estrella…"

LA MUSIK

vino un alemán
miró
e inmediatamente fundó el
Concentus Musicus Araucanus

un día agarré y dije
a lo mejor voy a escuchar un concierto

daban sonata en mi bemol
para dos arpas y siringa agreste

me puse el perramus de organza
y un chorro de extracto francés
que tengo desde la Primera Guerra Mundial

tomé el 106
me pasé una cuadra
no importa era temprano
el timbre del 106 hacía pío pío
una señora triste me preguntó ¿desciende?
no señora
yo bajo

rectrocedí una cuadra
cuando llegué solo quedaba
Paraíso tras la viga
y bueno
peor es nada y en polvo te convertirás

el programa decía ritornelli
cantorum danse macabre
y de nuevo decía ritornelli
para qué habré venido
y Kyrie Gloria

agarrate fuerte
es la cultura
lo cual significa:
que unos araban los campos y de allí salían plantas
y otros araban los encéfalos y de allí salían
los hermanos Karamazov

eso le dijeron a Cuqui
que sigue Letras

también le dijeron otras cosas
pero ya empezaba el concierto
y yo estoy aquí para relatar el concierto

a mí me encanta relatar conciertos
es mucho más cultural que pasar diapositivas
de Firenze y decir ¿te acordás Carlos
cuando perdiste un zapato en el Baptisterio?

por qué será
que los que tocan arpa siempre son mujeres

con túnicas verdes flanqueaban
al de la siringa
un flaco de negro
parecido a Leguisamo

no estaba mal el concierto
nada mal
el pizzicato es una beyeza
dijo el de al lado a la de más allá
y también dijo contrapunto ricercare
y timbre (el de 106 hace pío pío)
y añadió cantus firmus y Guillaume de Machaut

entretanto no sé por qué
el flaco de negro
parecido a Leguisamo
me recordó el casino
(diría "de Montecarlo" pero no sé mentir)
de Miramar

no va más ululaba Leguisamo
bajo los ritornelli de las fichas
la danse macabre del cero
y el tapete firmus firmus
como la roca Tarpeya   (es la cultura)
que hace rima con Pompeya   (es la cultura)
y con la rubia Mireya   (de *élite* y popular)

en fin
ustedes habrán visto
que la Musik no solo amansa a las fieras
sino que además
vuelve locos a los pollitos
favorece la asociación de ideas
y permite expandirse en un diván
para narrar el concierto

bueno
estoy muerta
y quiero divertirme

vamos
¿dónde está todo?

¿no hay nadie?

sí
sí
pasa un brillo por la ventana

estoy afuera
y vos adentro
jugás con el espejo

me tapás un ojo con sol

bien hecho
porque estoy muerta
y quiero divertirme

¿ya puedo entrar?
¿todavía no?

¿que espere?
¿como antes?
¿un poco más?

como antes

los espejos
el sol

yo afuera
vos adentro

¿no todavía?

ENTREACTO

y cuando ya no queda
por dónde remendarlas
y no protegen de la noche
del pavor brujo
de la muerte y sus bromas

y cuando ya no queda un
alma en quien vomitar
tu panes
tus condenas
tus armisticios y destituciones
tus manicomios
donde vendaste al mundo
con filacterias
de odio

en bombachas semirrojas
sangra tu corazón

(siete de velos:
colgá las medias
de las troneras se desploma el maná
hierve la pascua
la familias se frotan
las tribus se prosternan
clanes brindan con héroes
héroes con megasimios)

y cuando ya no queda
por dónde remendarlas
y se abren en jirones tus medusas
cruje el arcón de herrumbre
detrás del párpado

salta el resorte
por fin llegaste
en alas del vacío
vestida de conejito blanco

¿te acordás
de las noches de invierno
al sol radiante?
¿astro rey le decían?
no me contestes

como creíamos entonces:
"¿para qué perder tiempo?"
siglos apenas
y un manual de instrucciones
muy mal compaginado

y para no perderlo
—al tiempo—
fuimos de la mortaja
a la vejez
y de allí a la edad media

y para no perderlo
inventamos
la guerra santa
del roce de la lengua con los dientes
una tormenta palatal

y aún recuerdo
las casitas sin calle
los gatos triangulares
abstractos de hambre
alrededor del día

vos también te acordás
solo que te has adelantado tanto
mientras yo hablaba
que llegaste al babero
y empapás de sonido
las nieblas confortables

salud niñita

no te detengas a esperarme
la retórica es mi problema

cuando yo encuentre algún final feliz
—y casi lo encontré—
voy a trepar
a tu callar
para compartirlo

y si me quedan piernas
gatearé hasta mi cuna

MOHAMMED KAFKA LIBRERO

—¿*O Thyself?*
—agotado
100.000 ejemplares en dos meses
—¿y *Cowself?*
—en edición bilingüe
copto-húngaro
con el copto se puede
hay unos cursos
dicen que se parece mucho al québecois
claro
nada como *Cowself* en sajón medio
pero voló
lisa y llanamente
no ha quedado ni uno
puedo ofrecerle en cambio
el *Quijote* de Avellaneda
—¿cómo hago con *Cowself?*
—o porno complutense
siglo XII *you know*
después tengo en oferta
una partida de Arthur Hailey *Opera Omnia* en rústica
y *Las Vidas Paralelas Se Onanisman*
del Pseudo Plutonio y como si eso fuera poco
dos peines de bolsillo un sacacorcho una
estampita de Lutero

solo por el día de hoy

soy el pez chico

voy a tus dientes

todos los asuntos están en orden

no hay forma alguna de alterar mi destino
de refrán

llevo una entraña fecunda en
virus
mercurio
tus sabrosos bisnietos

soy el pez chico

ya llego

no hay forma alguna de alterar
tu destino
de refrán

SECUENCIA OCCIDENTAL HORROROSA CON FINAL CHINO ECUÁNIME

un nacer significa desear todo
y fastidiar y fastidiar

un crecer significa desear mucho
y fastidiarse y fastidiar

madurar significa desear algo
y fastidiar por no obtenerlo

viejecer significa desear poco
y fastidiar cada vez más

y molil significa deseal nada
y fastidial cada ve meno

KIKIRIKYRIE

dios nos ayude o dios no nos ayude
o nos ayude a medias
o nos haga creer que nos ayuda
y después mande decir que está ocupado
o nos ayude oblicuamente
con un piadoso "ayúdate a ti mismo"
o nos acune en brazos canturreando que vamos a cobrar
si no dormimos inmediatamente
o nos susurre que hoy estamos y mañana ay también
o nos cuente la historia de la mejilla
y la del prójimo y la del leproso
y la del muchacho lunático y la del mudo que habla
o se coloque los auriculares
o nos sacuda fuerte rugiendo que vamos a cobrar
si no nos despertamos inmediatamente
o nos haga el test del árbol
o nos lleve al zoológico a mirar
cómo nosotros nos miramos
o nos señale un viejo tren sobre un fantasma de puente
apuntalado por carteles de pañal descartable

dios nos ayude o no o a medias
o renqueando

dios nos
dios qué
o más o menos
o tampoco

La antología

¿tú eres
la gran poietisa
Susana Etcétera?
mucho gusto
me llamo Petrona Smith-Jones
soy profesora adjunta
de la Universidad de Poughkeepsie
que queda un poquipsi al sur de Vancouver
y estoy en Argentina becada
por la Putifar Comissión
para hacer una antología
de escritoras en vías de desarrolo
desarrolladas y también menopáusicas
aunque es cosa sabida que sea como fuere
todas las que escribieron y escribirán en Argentina
ya pertenecen a la generación del 60
incluso las que están en guardería
e inclusísimamente las que están en geriátrico

pero lo que me importa profundamente
de tu poesía y alredededores
es esa profesión —aaah ¿cómo se dice?—
profusión de íconos e índices
¿tú qué opinas del ícono?
¿lo usan todas las mujeres
o es también cosa del machismo?

porque tú sabes que en realidad
lo que a mí me interesa

es no solo que escriban
sino que sean feministas
y si es posible alcohólicas
y si es posible anoréxicas
y si es posible violadas
y si es posible lesbianas
y si es posible muy muy desdichadas

es una antología democrática
pero por favor no me traigas
ni sanas ni independientes

—¿dónde está la salida?
—¿perdón?
—le preguntaba dónde está la salida
—no
 no hay salida
—¿pero cómo si yo entré?
—claro
 yo la recuerdo
 además la estoy viendo
 pero salida
 salida no hay
 ¿vio?
—pero no puede ser
 voy a salir por donde entré
—no
 ya es muy tarde
 desde las diez hay entrada prohibida
 además ¿qué quiere? ¿que me den un lavado de cabeza
 dejando salir a una persona
 por la entrada?
—escúcheme
 tiene que haber un modo de llegar a la calle
—¿ya preguntó en informes?
—sí
 pero me mandaron a usted
—y bueno
 y yo le digo que no hay salida
—¿dónde hay un teléfono?
—¿para llamar a quién?
—a la policía
—esto es la policía

—¿pero está loco? si es una sala
de conciertos
—eso hasta cierta hora
después es la policía
—¿y qué me va a pasar?
—depende del comisario de turno
si le toca Loiácono
por ahí la saca barata
y en menos de unos días está afuera
—pero esto es una locura
¿dónde está la otra gente?
—sector de confinados
primer subsuelo
—¿por qué
hacen
esto?
—vamos tía
no me diga que nunca fue a un concierto

MURGATORIO

olé olé
olé olá
yo soy el nieto
de mi papá

olé olé
olé olá
voy al piscólogo
a investigar

por qué por qué
pour quoi pour quoi
la vie en rose
no es pour moi

tal vez tal vez
quizá quizá
esto hay que verlo en
profundidad

molta lettura
molta poesia
molta cultura
molta pazzia

Nevski Stogorny
Drugoi Igrushky
Gogol Andreiev
Chejov Tiburshky

y cuando supe
mis perspectivas
ya me encontraba
en la intensiva

hombre de ciencia
hombre de mundo
oh gran maestro
oh viejo inmundo

todo supiste
todo pudiste
mas ahora viste
que esto no es chiste

olé olé
olé olá
nadie con   testa en
el más
a

cá

ROUND 15

ah sí
fácil
word games
tampón de voces tales
mimpide
tra
gar

más fácil que no hacer
o hacer nada
como el tío de dios

como el tío de dios
que no hizo nada

volar delalf abeto

me ahogo

eso que se llamaba aquello
ahora es "esto"
alias "algo"
alias "la cosa"
y en el lapso que va de la segunda línea a la anterior
se ha trocado lo mismo por lo mismo
y "esto" sigue con más
con peróxido

un montón ululante de no sé qué
se ha juntado
frente a la iglesia

eso que se llamaba aquello
ahora es "esto"

y en el fin era el Nombre

LIBRETOS

I

rapsodia homericana

desde San Petersburgo
los Cuatro Grandes
rubrican otro armisticio
Simeón y Volodia son arrestados
por escribir *graffiti* con aerosoles
Simeón y Volodia son fusilados
en los salones de Castel Gandolfo
Su Santidad Papa
moscas mientras un chambelán
limpia fija y da esplendor
cunden viruela negra peste negra viuda negra
un vidente declara al *New York Times*
que tales epidemias se llamarán un día
viruela boba peste rosa y viuda alegre
otro vidente pronostica el retorno al futuro
Juan Cruz Montejo muere madura crece
nace en Paysandú
gateando en los corredores
los Cuatro Grandes
juegan con honda
yo-yo nuclear
genitales podados por la vieja
(esto se entenderá
dice el tercer vidente
cuando advenga un tal Sigmundo

o Segismundo)
en Glasgow nieva
en Túnez hay nubosidad variable
moscas d. C. Papa Su Santidad
en los jardines de Castel Gandolfo
trinan los cardenales por más y mejor
ira gula envidia soberbia lujuria
etcétera codicia y adulterio
en la quiniela gana el 666
desde las casamatas
los Cuatro Grandes
dan pase libre
a todo vatecónsul
y/o bardo-Nobel

mirá lo que hay en el cielo
no veo nada
mirá lo que hay en el suelo
no veo nada
mirá lo que hay en el agua en el fuego
no veo nada

en Troya sale el sol

no veo nada

II

la segunda partida

comienza
y comienza
y comienza

edad de la risa

dame un beso (vos)
contagiame (¡ya mismo! ¡ya!
¡zaguanes curvos del otro mundo!)

CONSUMA MÁS HOSTIA MÁS CRIMEN

teniendo en cuenta la extensión de la noche polar
Yo te habría dicho: No cantará el gallo
sin que me hayas negado trescientas veces tres

por otra parte —innecesario es recalcarlo—
fue lo que hiciste

claro que según A. Camus Yo me sabía responsable indirecto
del asunto de Herodes y "todos los niños menores de dos años
que había en Belén y en todos sus alrededores".
pero eso no te justifica
aunque en el fondo a quién le importa
el libreto es como es
hay que seguirlo

ahora prestame una lombriz

ahora prestame un beso en la mejilla
ahora meté la mano en mis gangrenas
ahora llorá
y ahora consolate
soñando que ya vuelvo
y *tus* horrendos sacrificios
te ganarán mi diestra

roca   roca
(sobre esta roca)
arenisca
Yo te abandono a los libretos del tiempo

III

la segunda espera

agotados los medios para obtener amor
(:elemento plegable en forma de pajarita
se alza la Vía Verdadera
cuyo tránsito no es fácil
pero sí inevitable
como es inevitable
sobrevivir a las b..bas
mirá los japoneses cucaracha
.ermanos del mundo
necesitamos mantas vacunas
aspiradoras . .che en polvo
. . . . famél . . . .
. . . . sitamos plasma rencor y whisky dietético

hermanos del mundo
bienhadados Abeles
necesitamos todo
excepto logos
. . . .
. . . .
erigir
. . . .
. . . .
ruina(s) . . . .
hacen de un mundo nuevo un
v. .erable emplazamiento
. . . . mos pa.
. . . . yoghurt
. . . .
cráteres en el mar . .tacumbas
nuevo . . . . a podrido
pestes flam . . . . .
más arte
más dep . . . .
. .ofesorado
más ironía, *darling*

de este Árbol
no elijas . . . . no hay historia
seguí el lib . . . .
picoteá de lo otro
vagina .ndeleble parí muertos
que construyan

Ova Completa: A Feast of Meaning

This book is an acid, a linguistic witches' sabbath, a diatribe against politically correct thinking. When Thénon published it in 1987, Argentina had only recently returned to democracy, leaving behind one of the bloodiest dictatorships in history.

Up to that time, poets had resisted the discourse (and the practices) of terror, entrenching themselves in an extreme condensation of language. They had found a way of saying more with less, eluding the pincers of censorship and its deadly risks. To the *desaparecidos*,[1] to the death flights,[2] to the policies that persecuted and abandoned the most vulnerable, they had answered with a kind of asthmatic syntax, made of taut phrases and spasmodic rhythms. Thénon herself had written *distancias,*[3] saturating the white space with meaning, opening subterfuges, making the poems dance across the page like skeletons or material ghosts.

Now, with the political opening, there was space to explore less gloomy terrain, to move toward play and insolence, and *Ova Completa* was, without a doubt, the most extreme example of this change.

---

1   From 1976 to 1983, Argentina was ruled by a military junta. During those years of state-sponsored terrorism, the junta persecuted people it suspected of being political dissidents aligned with leftist, socialist, or social justice causes. The junta clandestinely kidnapped, tortured, and killed an estimated 30,000 people, disposing of their bodies as a way of seeking impunity. These individuals came to be known as the *desaparecidos*, or "disappeareds."

2   "*Vuelos de la muerte*" were one of the methods used by the military junta to disappear people: victims were thrown alive, drugged, from aircraft into a river or the sea.

3   Susana Thénon, *distancias*, (Buenos Aires: Torres Agüero Editor, 1984); *distancias / distances*, the English translation by Renata Treitel, was published by Sun & Moon Press in 1994.

This book has everything: quotidian speech; cursing; utterances in Greek, Latin, French, and English; invectives; jargon (legal, soccer, racetrack, tango); references to the Malvinas War; sacrilege; scatology; sex; neologisms; free association; chaotic lists; temporal dislocation and furied attacks on every kind of cliché, including those that come from the paternalistic gazes of the Northern hemisphere.

> if you don't like "and my Peripherals"
> you can choose from these leftovers: "and my Kits"
>   "and my Gadgets"
>   "and my Accessories"
>   "and my Tassels"
>   "and my Replacements"
>   "and my Trinkets"
>   "and my Chess Pieces"
>   "and my Agoraphobics"

It could be said that, in Thénon's gesture, language is a stammering puppet, full of sonic contaminations, always on the point of veering off, from one letter to another, from one seme to another, from one idea to another. Or even—and which amounts to the same thing—that in that indecipherable and carnivalesque that unfolds in writing, a syntactic explosion weaves dispersion together with fortuitous encounter, in order to impede any attempt at homogenous discourse.

I repeat: *Ova Completa* is a ferocious assault on social, formal, genre, and gender conventions. A true consciousness of language that is exacerbated, if it's possible, with the use of irony, often self-directed.

> taking a chance with "wrecked" or "incontinent"
> it's a passport to marginality

whilst you want to be the prize of crackpot anthologies?
to have a wart in the curriculum?

Perhaps this explains why the book had, at the very moment of its release, such an enthusiastic reception on the part of the new generations of poets. *Ova Completa* was read and appreciated in all its splendor, in all is aggressive seriousness, in all its hilarious novelty. I don't think it's absurd to claim that Thénon opened the way for what was known later in the Argentine poetry scene as the "poetry of the 90s," on the condition that it is remembered that she arrived at desacralization and colloquial outburst *after* an arduous path of semantic and formal condensation, and that the presumed "triviality" of her discourse was always unfailingly political, visceral, and genuine.

*

"The poem is concerned with everything, even the most ungrateful earth," Susana Thénon wrote.[4]

Maybe because of this, in that obsessive arc that goes from *Edad sin tregua* (1958) to *Ova completa* (1987), the "strange places" are repeated as signs that allude to the "tragic and tender expiration of language," understood as that "minimum distance that exists between us and ourselves, or between ourselves and the other,"[5] to say the mark of every solitude, estrangement, or uprootedness.

There is in this work, it seems, a geography that turns outward in order to immerse itself in the abyss of what isn't seen, what is ignored or silenced for reasons of taste or good manners, perhaps in the confidence that only a

---

4   See Ana María Barrenechea, "La documentación marginal para *distancias* de Susana Thénon," *Filología* 27 (1994): 79-80.

5   Thénon says this in relation to *distancias* in a letter from February 17, 1968 to Ana María Barrenechea included in *La morada imposible, vol. 2* (Buenos Aires: Ediciones Corregidor, 2004), 193.

deformed map can yield the skeleton of a soul. The sensation is one of being lost, of the painful loving of what's been abolished. Always one more step. Always an intervening crack, like a fold where it is possible to go to look for what the poems can't explain, but can understand.

These will be poems for poetry, she wrote, trying to explain how she wrote.

And in one sense, they are. Poems unrefined, debased, erect like a monument in a black sun world, like music boxes or sonic homelands. As if the objective of the process were to stage the always unrealizable project of meaning, to remember that, as Severo Sarduy said, the desiring language of poetry doesn't recognize functionality, transgresses the useful, insists on failure. This is desire *par excellence*, a desire for what does not exist, blind and in the void, bringing forth the impossible: a feast of meaning.

If the seed of this conception of the world-as-enigma and language-as-blindness is present from the beginning, it is in *Ova Completa* that it reaches the climax of its corrosive ability. There, the carnivalesque zeal—that multiplies the profanations and palimpsests—gives as a result a language that, exhausting intertextuality and parody, intensifies the boustrophedonic character of the poem to its very limits. The effect is one of radical estrangement. As if the signs (not the emotions) revealed a disequilibrium between the experience and the world that only a stark music, ambivalent, could transcribe. And yes. What could be better for unexpressing reality— that opacity that needs to be spoken—than a music made of familiarly unrecognizable particles like Stockhausen's *Mikrophonie*, halfway between crystal architecture and the mysteries of a film still?

It's almost unnecessary to add that the author of *Ova Completa* draws on both "vulgar" and "refined" language equally. Aristophanes, Apuleius, Catullus, Boccaccio, Pietro Aretino, Rabelais, Góngora, and Joyce are her masters. Undoubtedly, Girondo's *En la masmédula*—that, in the style of the phonetic mosaics of Haroldo de Campos, invents, pluralizes, or superimposes words, providing a spectacle of a split subjectivity—deserves to figure in the list of precursor texts. Also, of course, the "very cacophonous little music" of Alejandra Pizarnik's *La bucanera de Pernambuco o Hilda la Polígrafa*. Although the parallels between the two poets hasn't yet been noted, it is obvious that they share various textual procedures (the sexual charge of the signifier, the degradation of culture, the mix of speech registers, the deformation of Latin, or banal usage), even though, in Thénon, the coarseness is always kept at a less intense coordinate, the lyricism is absent, and the obscene has a more acidic appearance, at times, more political.

As if united with what was lost, her voice speaks to say nothing, or better to say, to be the voice of what is absent. There is no other world, it seems to affirm, because there is no world. Or even, in words the order of death always sings, that is to say, has already been sung. It is better to abandon the expressible (that exiles us from ourselves) and then remain unsheltered, in those arid landscapes where the roofless house of poetry is, its center unplaceable and in a hurry to conquer precarity, its trembling of nightmares and light.

Poet and spy, Susana Thénon (1935–1991) dreamed of a literature that could fit in the hollow of a child's hand. Her aim always consisted of not giving accounts, of running suddenly to the encounter with the splinters of the self to fulfill loss, not to cancel it, to shine on it like a lighthouse.

María Negroni
Buenos Aires, May 2020
tr. Silvina López Medin and Rebekah Smith

THE WHOLE OVA

By the time you're reading this, the knot in my stomach will hopefully have gone away, or subsided, or at least transitioned to being less permanently present. It is a 2020 generalized knot of anxiety, probably, but it is also a knot that has tightened as I finalize and release this translation of *Ova Completa* into the world. I have been living with these poems, reading and re-reading, translating and re-translating, for five years. Sometimes I think I could keep at it for at least another five. There are some decisions I still worry about ever making. Decision-making is, for me, one of the hardest things, and so I often think it is strange that I have translated at all. The number of choices of sound, rhythm, and meaning called for in any single poem can be overwhelming. And each decision multiplies: sending the manuscript to friends and editors for comments at each stage of the process was to return to the questioning all over again—and on and on it goes.

This book is called *Ova Completa* because for all the years I have sat with these poems, with this book, no other English title has seemed so sufficiently apt. "Ova" is no more a Spanish word than an English one, except in that Spanish is considered a Latinate language and English is not. "Completa," of course, is also not an English word, but is surely recognizable—drawing up ideas of fullness and completion, of an entire collection, and thus a sense of completion, of fulfillment. And yet the poems themselves undermine this idea of wholeness. Within Susana Thénon's book, there are multitudes, but not an entire system, nothing to completely fill the space she creates as she uses language to destroy the structures which frame the world in which we exist. Instead, there is a kind of "done-up chaos," as she calls it, a "chaos that can smile, a chaos that can cry."[1]

---

1 "Susana Thénon: Maquillando el caos," interview with Mirta Rosenberg and Diana Bellessi, *Diario de Poesía*, no. 11 (1988): 3-4.

The title itself does some of the work of this destruction with its multilingual word play that is further developed and clarified in the poem also called "Ova Completa." The play makes use of the functions of the dictionary while undermining any claim it might make to some absolute semantic truth. The title, "Ova Completa," (literally, *Ova*: "egg" or "ova"; and *Completa*: "full" or "complete") is footnoted at the bottom of the page where Thénon provides "translations" of the two words from Latin to Spanish. The dictionary-styled definitions with their grammatical parts of Latin speech make a claim on authority with their form, though Thénon's humorous use of the form points to her distrust of this authority. "Ova," here in the footnote, are "huevos" (*eggs*); and "completa" is "colmado" (*abundant*). While these definitions are correct, they are but only one part of any truth. She chooses the specific "huevos" and "colmado" in order to make explicit the reference to an expression that most Argentine readers would have already recognized: "huevos llenos," or "tener los huevos llenos." This expression is literally "to have full balls," which in Argentine slang means "to be fed up." Thénon re-genders the expression with her *ova*, telling us that it is she, a woman, who is fed up. Fed up with *what* is pointed to but not explicitly explained in the poem, or in the book—and in a book with so many points of reference and critique, it cannot and should not be reduced to a single idea or problem.

Here and throughout the book, Susana Thénon's clever multi-layered play on words, genders, definitions, and written authority make clear that whatever the narrator or author is fed up with, she is here to trouble what we think we know about power and society and our roles within and views from these structural frames. And so, *Ova Completa* performs a two-pronged assault with both form and content: against literary canons and established poetic, linguistic, and semantic forms; and against patriarchal and colonial methods of control. By foregrounding the female, Thénon claims for us a valid status: a woman, insisting on her right to exist, naming and occupying a position within societal frames whose very substance is made up of the conditions by which she is erased. Despite the violence and sardonic humor, Thénon's poetry insists itself into life, joyously exposing the edges of the frames of structures of power to show how they are selective, how they are edited. Her work propels forward its own radical sexualized sovereignty of self, one that perhaps exists within the frame but does not accept it, constantly exceeds it, and in so doing offers a set of strategies of resistance to it.

*

There is so much more I want to tell you about this book, about the poems and about the process of translating them. There is perhaps too much. I want to tell you about practicalities, about how some of these poems felt impossible to translate, but how here, in this book and with this English translation, we're interested in something other than the merely possible, I hope.

I want to tell you, for example, that I couldn't find a way that didn't seem incredibly problematic to mirror the Chinese accent Thénon uses in "Poem with Equanimous Chinese Ending," so I went with an approach that relied on a superficial understanding of classical Chinese philosophy, in which the end of life is a welcoming of non-desire, a less fussy time; but that I did allow the Argentine accent to come into English as she uses it, in the poem "Y Vos También." I, additionally, translated her English title of that poem ("And So Are You") to Spanish as well, though I leave other of her English titles in English. Doing so allowed the entry of "vos" (a term used in Argentina and a few other Latin American countries) for "you" into the translated poem, and this poem that is playing with both the Argentine accent and English syntax seemed particularly open to admitting this reverse translation.

What to do, generally, with Thénon's use of English, laced throughout the text to both comedic and dramatic ends? During the Malvinas War with

England in 1982, it was forbidden to play music in English on the radio in Argentina, and so Thénon's appropriation of this additional colonial language into her poems gives the book a transgressive charge that cannot be replicated by, say, translating those phrases back into Spanish. I have chosen for the most part to keep the English in English—sometimes italicized, sometimes not, as she did—but I do use some Spanish in places where I thought it could *point* to the way Thénon brought English into her work—for reasons of gendered language, common usage, or translational logic.

As for those italics, sometimes Thénon uses them for languages other than Spanish (but not always), sometimes she uses them to show multiple speakers (but not always), and sometimes she uses them to quote songs or cultural references (but not always). Since her italics don't map neatly onto one system, I have tended to follow her usage, but there is a time or two where the italics in my translation get a bit unruly themselves, slipping between her poem and my translation, intending to play—as she does—on the multiplicity of voices and registers in the poems, without ever resolving their intention. Given her mixing of languages, registers, and forms, I often felt it was best—instead of aiming for representational exactitude in the English—to try to translate the play as much as the letter.

And she plays so much. That was one of the most exciting challenges of translating these poems. It felt like an opportunity and invitation to have fun with English in a manner akin to her play with Spanish, as well as with all the other languages and accents she brings in. There are the gendered adjectives and nouns Thénon uses throughout the book—words that carry gender in their form, even without an explicit subject, creating an effect that cannot be fully recreated in English. At the end of the poem "As Time Goes By," for example, are words that refer to men ("confusing") and women ("unpublished," "unjustly forgotten") that didn't feel possible to clearly gender in English. While my solution seems unsatisfactory at times, it also felt important to keep the stark list in English. Thénon exercises a punning, interlingual, and gendered humor, alongside emphasizing sounds both repeated and inverted. Rather than focus on directly translating the words at all points, I tried too to engage with similar concerns in the English poems.

There is more to say, and it seems to me that there may always be more to say. At times over these years, I have felt very close to Thénon as I worked so intimately with her words and sounds. At other times, she has seemed inscrutable—opaque perhaps—in a way that still allowed me entry, although there is surely much about these poems I still don't understand. I made some choices, I made some decisions, and I think I made some interesting and challenging poems in English, although it makes me nervous still to imagine them as "finished." In fact, they're not finished.

Rebekah Smith
Brooklyn, NY, September 2020

Translator's Acknowledgments

As with all things, this translation is far from a solo undertaking. There are many people who have helped this book come to be, who have supported and encouraged and pushed and cheered over the years, and I could not have done any of this without them.

First I must thank poet Daniel Durand for introducing me to Susana Thénon's work, to *Ova completa*, so many years ago in his studio in Once, Buenos Aires—he thought I would love her work and I did. Not too long after, as soon as she heard I was thinking about translating some of the book, Silvina López Medin became this project's biggest advocate. She has encouraged publication, connected dots, and answered more questions than I even knew I had. This book would not exist without her erudite and enthusiastic commitment to Thénon's work.

Thank you to María Fernanda Pampín at Corregidor Editions for granting permission to publish the translation, and to María Negroni, for supporting the project from the beginning as well as contributing an illuminating contextualization of Thénon's work.

Many, many thanks go to Victoria Cóccaro and Emma Wipperman, who gave astute editorial suggestions throughout various stages of this translation. Thanks to Sara Cipani, Thomas Hilder, David Larsen, Cameron Pearson, JD Pluecker, and Asiya Wadud who offered varieties of support—linguistic and otherwise—to this work over the years. Thomas Hilder also generously offered me a quiet residency in Berlin where I completed much of this translation, and Marcos Perearnau and Barbara Molinari, at La Sede in Buenos Aires, offered an early home to my work on this project. At NYU, Andrea Gadberry, Fred Moten, and Cristina Vatulescu have all offered valuable feedback on my writing and thinking about Thénon's work, which in turn has made my revisions of the translations more rigorous and thorough. I thank all of them for all they have offered to help this project on its way.

Some of these translated poems appeared in the *Brooklyn Rail*, *A Perfect Vacuum*, *Poesía en acción* on the Action Books blog, and the *Washington Square Review*. I thank the editors of these publications for including Thénon's work. Thank you to Mónica de la Torre, Terrance Hayes, and Sylvia Molloy for reading advance copies and offering kind words of praise. Ruby Kapka, wizard of all she chooses to do, designed the cover based on wild and at times incoherent desires, and for that I could not be more grateful. I read some translations of these poems at Madeleine Braun's 251 Throop Avenue Reading Series, and at Sam Bett and Todd Portnowitz's Us&Them series at Molasses Books, and I thank these organizers for the space to first bring these versions to the public. Thank you to the New York State Council on the Arts for a grant that supported the completion of this translation.

And finally thank you to everyone at Ugly Duckling Presse for making this book a reality, and for sustaining me and this project with their unwavering enthusiasm. In particular, I would like to thank Sarah Lawson and Lee Norton for much of the necessary behind the scenes work that makes books like this happen, and Lee for additional late-stage edits; Matvei Yankelevich, for many things, often, especially for early and ongoing trust in me and my work, and here particularly for insightful editorial comments and helping me think through the translation of the title; and finally, the true champions of this book: Silvina López Medin and Daniel Owen, whose keen editorial eyes and swift and tireless responses to my doubts and questions made this book better than I could ever have imagined.

Lastly, I thank you all so, so much for reading, and I thank Susana Thénon for writing these poems.

Ugly Duckling Presse's Lost Literature Series publishes neglected, never-before-translated, or scarcely available works of poetry and prose, and resonant historical works that fall outside these confines.

1   Gabriel Pomerand, *Saint Ghetto of the Loans*
2   Vito Acconci, Bernadette Mayer, *0 to 9: The Complete Magazine*
3   Aram Saroyan, *Complete Minimal Poems*
4   Paul Scheerbart, *The Development of Aerial Militarism*
5   Su Shi, *East Slope*
6   Jack Micheline, *One of a Kind*
7   Carlos Oquendo de Amat, *5 Meters of Poems*
8   Manuel Maples Arce, *City: Bolshevik Super-Poem in 5 Cantos*
9   Guillevic, *Geometries*
10 Ernst Herbeck, *Everyone Has a Mouth*
11 Heimrad Bäcker, *Seascape*
12 Alejandra Pizarnik, *Diana's Tree*
13 César Vallejo & César González-Ruano, *Vallejo: Heraldo de Madrid*
14 Alejandra Pizarnik, *The Most Foreign Country*
15 Hirato Renkichi, *Spiral Staircase: Collected Poems*
16 Marosa di Giorgio, *I Remember Nightfall*
17 Constance DeJong, *Modern Love*
18 Eleni Vakalo, *Before Lyricism*
19 Laura Riding, *Experts are Puzzled*
20 Laura Riding, *Convalescent Conversations*
21 Marcel Duchamp, Henri-Pierre Roche, Beatrice Wood, *The Blind Man*
22 Arnaldo Calveyra, *Letters So That Happiness*
23 Omar Cáceres, *Defense of the Idol*
24 Amanda Berenguer, Materia Prima
25 Paul Nougé, Paul Colinet, Louis Scutenaire, *Ideas Have No Smell: Three Belgian Surrealist Booklets*
26 Alejandra Pizarnik, *A Tradition of Rupture*
27 Alejandra Pizarnik, *The Last Innocence / The Lost Adventure*
28 Laura Riding, *The Close Chaplet*
29 Bobbie Louise Hawkins, *One Small Saga*
30 Åke Hodell, *The Marathon Poet*
31 Ulises Carrión, *Sonnet(s)*
32 Susana Thénon, *Ova Completa*
33 Vasily Kamensky, *Tango with Cows*